Book Description

Raise your hand if yo□ □□□□□□□□ en't sure. Perhaps you're □ □□□□□□□□ bed; these are all symptoms of depression. Maybe you gu□ □□□ □□ □□ for you or someone you know. Either way, a good idea to have this book around for when trouble comes and you feel exhausted and stressed. It contains several ingredients you can use to devise coping strategies, develop self-care, and relieve anxiety.

Ebony Summersett explains that depression can be confusing, but it's not as mysterious as people think. Though the severity of depression varies from person to person, the feeling of depression of self is not uncommon. The problem isn't all in our heads; it affects the whole person. And as depression affects all parts of our bodies, so does the healing.

The Mental Health Cookbook teaches how to:

- Use key ingredients to deal with chronic unhappiness.
- Get to the bottom of the causes of your anxiety and how a chemical imbalance affects our minds and emotions.
- Find out how you may be negatively affected by these invisible emotions.
- Discover how to get rid of harmful patterns of behavior, like having a lack of boundaries.
- Discover healing answers in your subconscious mind.
- Put an end to depression, and become the healthiest, happiest version of yourself.

Ebony Summersett offers much-needed relief to anyone who wishes to free themselves from the depressive cycle and rediscover their inner well-being. Read on if you want that to be you!

THE MENTAL HEALTH COOKBOOK

*Self Help Guide in Understanding and
Managing Anxiety and Depression*

Ebony Summersett

TABLE OF CONTENTS

INTRODUCTION

"The only constant in life is change."

- Heraclitus

Even if we are certain to change our life, we often find ourselves unprepared for the chaos that comes with it. While we progress through life stages, it is important to learn how to manage our emotions as we move through difficult times.

One of the most difficult emotions to manage, however, is depression. People often associate depression with sadness. They think that depression is a crying person dressed in black. However, most people with depression will hide behind a mask. They tend to wear a "brave face" as they struggle to get through the day. They don't want to burden their family or friends with their problems.

Sadness is one of the strongest emotions in the kaleidoscope of human experiences. This can easily develop into depression, especially by terrible events that are hard to understand, such as going through a divorce or watching a newscast featuring survivors of mass shootings. In the beginning, it will be difficult, but eventually, the kaleidoscope will begin to change.

In the United States, major depression ranks as one of the most common mental disorders according to the National Institute of Mental Health (2019). Some people with major depression experience significant impairments, which can make daily activities difficult or impossible. It is often challenging for a clinically depressed person to see their feelings because their numbness is so intense.

It's normal to feel down sometimes. Women, for example, may experience a change in mood after a recent birth, during their premenstrual cycle, or at the start of menopause. But sometimes, the cause is due to an imbalance of chemicals in our brains versus a significant life event.

Is there nothing to be done then? No! There are many things we can do to improve our emotional states. For example, like our heart or lungs, our brains are an organ and exercise can help to keep them healthy and strong. Anxiety can be reduced or even eliminated by learning to master your emotions.

This book will teach you how to regulate your emotional body, your mind, and your body. You will learn practices that are effective in mastering your feelings and finding peace. This book is not intended to replace your therapy, medical assistance, and medication regime. You can use it in conjunction with what you're already doing. We aim to provide you with knowledge, skills, and experiences on how to effectively deal with emotions in a way that does not negatively affect your quality of life.

In the long run, you will see a significant difference in your ability to deal with the chaos around you if you are open to trying the exercises in this book. The idea of change will no longer be a burden, but a blessing.

THE DEEP DISH OF ANXIETY
AND DEPRESSION

"A human being can survive almost anything, as long as she sees the end in sight. But depression is so insidious and it compounds daily, making it impossible to ever see the end. That fog is like a cage without a key."

- Elizabeth Wurtzel

If you're reading this book, you or someone you know likely relates to that quote. They've found themselves trapped in the deep dish of anxiety and depression; this is one pie that we could do without! But what's happening inside?

The most well-known cause of depression and anxiety is a chemical imbalance in the brain, most often caused by a hormone imbalance. This happens when there is too much or not enough of a hormone released from the endocrine system. Hormone imbalances can worsen conditions such as insomnia, mood fluctuations, anxiety, depression, or insomnia. But why does this happen?

The main reason is that the nerve cells of the brain communicate through neurotransmitters. You've probably heard of one of them: serotonin. Science has found that lack of it is often associated with depression, anxiety, and obsessive disorders.

But if we're looking at the physiological factors to depression and anxiety, we need to pay attention to a particularly important chemical that can make women vulnerable to poor mental health: estrogen. Estrogen plays an important role in maintaining a balanced mental state by keeping several neurotransmitters (such as dopamine, norepinephrine, and serotonin) in balance.

To create serotonin, the body's natural mood stabilizer and anti-depressant are needed. When levels of estrogen drop (like before menstruation), people are particularly vulnerable to mood disorders; this is because estrogen and serotonin are linked. As estrogen and serotonin levels rise, however, moods improve. This can be particularly frustrating for women as they have to go through this monthly when they are menstruating. The menstrual cycle can cause women to swing from crying spells to angry outbursts and anxiety attacks in a single day, only to return to their normal emotional state immediately afterward. It's an emotional rollercoaster.

Not all women may experience the same symptoms of estrogen fluctuations and low mood. Miller and Rogers, authors of "The Estrogen-Depression Connection," assert that women's sensitivity to estrogen changes is the major cause of depression rather than estrogen changes themselves. High estrogen levels during pregnancy may improve mood (Borst, 2021). Following conception, estrogen levels in a mother's body drop, resulting in a reduction in serotonin levels in the brain. Often, this is the catalyst for postpartum depression. At the same time, low estrogen levels also increase the risk of anxiety and depression during perimenopause.

However, depression and anxiety are rarely simple things. They are also, arguably more commonly, caused by life events.

CHAPTER 1: WHICH CAME FIRST, THE CHICKEN OR THE EGG

"I do believe in the old saying, 'What does not kill you makes you stronger.' Our experiences, good and bad, make us who we are. By overcoming difficulties, we gain strength and maturity."

- Angelina Jolie

It has long been a topic of debate as to whether depression is hereditary. There is no doubt that depression involves a change in brain chemistry, so it's reasonable to think that there is an identified biological reason for it—but is that reason set from birth? All we can really speak about are environmental factors that can trigger depression, like our upbringing.

The experiences we have, in our past and in our future, create us. Some are small ingredients, like sprinkling cinnamon over cookies; others are instrumental, like eggs in a meringue. These experiences have the greatest effect on our mental and physical health. But like ingredients in a recipe, the better we understand their sources and functions, the better the food will be.

It's impossible to list all the different life-changing events, either positive or negative. I've found it easier to categorize some of their common scars, the roots of mental illness and the ingredients to ourselves. Boubeau (2010), a world-renowned therapist, identifies five basic emotional scars: rejection, abandonment, humiliation, injustice, and betrayal. Keep in mind that these are often inflicted during childhood, and so are frequently unconscious wounds. It's also possible to have more than one of these wounds; we can still heal them.

1. ***Abandonment:*** The most obvious cause of this scar is being physically abandoned, but it's important to note

that it's not always the case. Those who have the abandonment scar lived feeling ignored, unsupported, misunderstood, and emotionally lonely. As a result, they believe they need others to be happy. They can't imagine themselves accomplishing something by themselves. In connection with that wound, there is a constant feeling of sadness, emptiness, and uncertainty.

2. **Betrayal:** The wound of betrayal is similar to the wound of abandonment, except for this: betrayal opposes loyalty. Here, the wounded person felt like someone was on their side and then switched. A sense of loss might result from this; a loss of trust, happy memories you have of someone, a loss of the future you imagined together. People who suffer the pain of betrayal often express: "I was disappointed, I was lied to, my trust was betrayed, I was used." They continue to feed the belief that they cannot trust anyone and should not commit to anyone because it hurts. Vulnerability is one of their weaknesses. The most common emotions felt by those who suffer from betrayal wounds are apathy, impatience, alertness, contempt, and distrust.

3. **Humiliation:** Whenever someone is degraded, ridiculed, or subdued, the emotion of humiliation is forced upon them. When someone bears the humiliation wound, they often felt discouraged from pursuing their desires; they felt they had to shrink back to be safe. These people also tend to nurture the limiting belief that they are worthless, that they are not worthy of happiness and don't deserve to be beautiful. As a result, they can have self-destructive behaviors because they often unconsciously choose to be unhappy in life. Humiliation wounds fill people with emotions such as contempt, shame, guilt, and disgust.

4. **Rejection:** Rejection wounds make a person feel less than human, because they feel like they've been tossed out or exchanged for a better option. An emotional wound of re-

jection will feed the unconscious mantra, "I'm unlovable, unacceptable, and unwanted." Although this mantra and its limiting beliefs may not be intentional, they result from the sense that the person isn't entitled to live their lives, be loved, or be happy.

5. ***Injustice:*** Injustice wounds occur when people feel like justice hasn't been served correctly, and as a result, they've been deeply wronged. As a result, they often feel unvalued, disrespected, and unappreciated. This causes them to see and expect the worst in the people around them; they believe the world is against them, and that they must be perfect before they can be given affection. Additionally, they often consider emotions to be negative. Victims also commonly believe that nothing is their fault, that the world just doesn't accept them and they don't belong. In addition to anger and contempt, disgust is also sometimes expressed through criticism and jealousy.

Unfortunately, these scars can be caused by about one billion different things. Whether the wound was inflicted once or repeated, whether the victim was young or old, whether the pain was intentional or not, all of these can cause depression and anxiety. They leave our minds panicking about the future and haunted by the past; however, they are the key to overcoming it as well.

But when we acknowledge the "ingredients" of our mental illness (though I only mentioned a few), we're able to learn how to cope with and grow through them. It's not a matter of hacking away at the root of a dandelion, though much like dandelions, we wish we weren't plagued by mental illness. With mental illness, you use the ingredient to better understand how to cope in the future. That way, when future events trigger depression or anxiety, you're armed with understanding and ready to live through it. They will no longer be able to control you.

Maybe you already know what life event brought you to this place in your mental health; if so, then the following exercise could at least be therapeutic. If, however, you're having trouble nailing down one particular event, then the exercise is very important to complete. Don't worry though! It's not difficult; it's only a recipe to understanding yourself.

How to Name Past Traumas

Time: As much as you need, but plan for at least 30 minutes to start.

Ingredients:

- A quiet, uninterrupted place (like a bedroom, car, park)
- 1 notebook, with a pen or pencil

Directions:

1. Go to a quiet place where you're unlikely to be interrupted. Get comfortable, and leave any distractions (eg, phones, pagers, iPods) in another place, or at least in a bag where they won't bother you. You may set a 30-minute timer to start; you can go over 30 minutes, but not less.
2. Close your eyes and think of the most common negative emotions you feel. Is it anger? loneliness? sadness? hopelessness? numbness? Write each of those down, preferably on separate pages.
3. One at a time, think back to the most recent time you felt that emotion. Where in your body do you feel it most? Is it heavy on your lungs? Tangled in your stomach? Write as detailed a description as you can; no one is here to judge you.
4. Now think about when was it the most intense? Did it hit you suddenly, like a flash of fire? Or did it develop slowly, like a glacier moving? Write about that experience.

5. Take a moment now and think about how often you feel this way? Is there a physical description you can give it? Is it more red or blue? Is there a sound that matches it? Maybe trumpets, violins, or cymbals?
6. Answer these questions for every emotion you listed.

Hopefully, this will not only show you a general source for the emotion, but it will help invest time in understanding that emotion. Once you know why you feel a certain way, and you understand that our feelings are neutral (it's our behavior that's either good or bad), then you'll be able to move forward, prepared for future emotions and how to cope with them.

Now that you've identified some sources of your past traumas, we can examine your current relationships. We need to see if they are healthy and growing; it's extremely difficult to heal one's mental illness if one is held back by unhealthy relationships. The following exercise will guide you through the process.

Recipe to Uncover Past and Current Traumas

You can soothe your nerves if you're feeling anxious by using your senses, such as taste, sight, smell, sound, and touch. With aromatherapy, you can relax and improve your mood through the use of scented candles.

Time: 20-40 minutes; this will vary from person to person.

Ingredients:

- 1 notebook, with a pen or pencil
- A few scented candles, and they don't have to be anything fancy. They can be your favorite scent or one of the following suggestions:
  - Lavender: Boosts physical and mental relaxation instantly.
  - Clary sage: Is beneficial for reducing symptoms of menopause, anxiety, and stress.

- o   Vanilla: Boosts feelings of happiness and promotes relaxation.
- o   Cinnamon: Provides a feeling of freshness and alertness, improves memory, and boosts mental clarity.
- o   Peppermint: De-stresses and energizes you, relieves stress, and eases nervous disorders.
- o   Any other natural scent, such as frankincense, sandalwood, lemon, and apple.

Directions:

1. Light a candle with a soothing smell and lie on your bed, resting your arms gently on top of your stomach. Breathe in for three seconds, then breathe out for three seconds. Do this at least five times.
2. While doing your deep breathing, imagine that you are having a peaceful night at home. Then let's introduce your friends. Picture each of them entering the house, and you smile at each of them. Is there one that you aren't particularly happy to see? Is there an unresolved conflict between the two of you?
3. Now picture your family arriving. Are all of them there? Is there someone in particular that hasn't arrived, like your father who has yet again disappointed you? How do you feel? Repeat the same with your colleagues, children, partner, and all the people in your life.
4. The party continues. Imagine yourself talking and hanging out with all of them. Is there a common problem with all of them? A sense of not being respected, understood, or left out? Is this similar to any pains that you experienced when you think of your family?
5. Visualize how you would like to resolve the problems currently existing in your relationships. Do you need to forgive anyone or apologize to someone? Picture how it would feel if you made peace. Do you see yourself feeling better? If it's a family member, do you see yourself being willing to go home more often for holidays? Think of all

the possibilities of joy and happiness in your life. Do you feel like there's a problem that can't be solved? What is it?

6. Take the pen and write all these feelings and past events, noting what you envision for the relationships in your life. Take note of how the relationships make you feel right now.

7. You may also use the flame of your candle as something to focus on while meditating in order to reduce stress even further. You can do these exercises staring into the light and doing deep breathing exercises.

CHAPTER 2: TRIGGERS

Anxiety sufferers know well that sometimes their panic falls out of the blue; sometimes it just seems to pop up out of nowhere. This can happen with any mental illness, where there may be a sudden rise in depressive or anxious thoughts, which leave you feeling overwhelmed. Although it can be hard to understand your mental illness and its causes, the more you understand it, the better you can manage it so it won't become paralyzing. Part of that is identifying what situations and actions that contribute to an onset of an anxious or depressive episode. These are what we refer to as triggers.

Anything can really be a trigger; it all depends on your trauma and mental illness. With that being said, the following is a list of common triggers, why they may be triggers, and how to know if they're your triggers. Keep track of which ones apply to you, and we'll discuss in the next chapter why that information is useful.

1. Social Interactions

This is one of the most well-known triggers in mental health. People suffering from anxiety often experience greater anxiety at social events or performing in front of others. It is difficult, however, to completely avoid each of these in everyday life. It's guaranteed that teachers will call on students and friends will always celebrate their birthdays or have parties. However, there are three individual triggers under the umbrella of "social interactions."

1. Meeting new people

Some people are particularly triggered by meeting new

people, and they become overwhelmed by what is the "right" thing to say or do. They spiral quickly when trying to interact with someone unfamiliar, as they are trying to guess what the other person is thinking of them.

2. Crowds

Others find crowds of people to be their trigger. They don't have an issue with one-on-one interactions, but the noise, movement, and lack of space in a throng of people drives them into the panic zone.

3. Pressured situations

This is a broad term that can describe both things like performing for people and trying to count out exact change for a cashier as a line builds behind you. Basically, any situation where a person is made to feel pressured to be perfect and/or as fast as possible triggers that person into a mental health spiral.

A person with social anxiety disorder is likely to think negatively about themselves and what events will transpire in social situations. They will often feel like people won't like them, or that they're bound to say or do something that will leave them embarrassed. Anxiety can be worse if you believe social situations are dangerous or threatening. When they step into a social situation, they spiral, becoming overwhelmed with uncertainty about what's happening, what they should say, what they should do, and how people are perceiving them. When they go home, they are exhausted (physically and emotionally) and they replay every potentially embarrassing interaction. The thought of returning to the public leaves them shaking with dread.

For depression sufferers, social interactions have a different implication. When one's emotions are numbed, and one sees others apparently enjoying themselves, one begins to think they are broken. This may turn into self-loathing; alternatively, they may feel like the world is shoving unattainable happiness in their face, which makes them want to avoid society even more.

2. Money Problems

Finances can trigger anxious or depressive episodes, whether it's over the pressure to save enough for retirement, feeling obligated to pay bills on time, or getting out of debt. The anxiety associated with finances extends beyond simply monitoring your account balance. As a result, irritability, tension and worried thoughts are apparent. You'll sometimes see people neglect checking their finances, think about what would happen if they ran short of money, or become overly vigilant about saving for rainy days.

This is a particular trigger of mine; I became obsessed with money at an early age. When I was a child, money equated to freedom since I came from a poor family. The lack of money irked me, and I was desperate for it. It became clear to me that those with it had an improved chance of success than I did. Besides having better clothes, toys, and food, they were also able to travel, go on school trips, and be part of a life outside of school that I was not able to experience because our budget was not there.

In my teens, I began working as my friends were in bed after a night out. Being in need of money means growing up fast, it was one more freedom that I didn't have, the freedom to decide what to do with my time. Yet with each new job, I was able to deal with many of my problems, but I lost any and all personal time. I felt that I was only a cog in a machine, not a person. Though my rent was paid, I wasn't able to enjoy it; I could only work.

How great would it be if your money brought you more happiness? But eventually we must realize that our experiences in life have the greatest impact, not the things we purchase. I learned that instead of comparing your purchases with those of your friends, it's better to try to create memorable shared experiences. Having less regret will result in happier spending and longer-lasting happiness.

3. Family Relations

Conflicts with spouses, parents, siblings, and other family members may trigger anxiety for some people. Visiting friends and family over Christmas is usually very exciting, but sometimes it can be suffocating. It's not uncommon to feel nervous or anxious about seeing your family or friends. You may even worry about having a panic attack or anxious about how someone will treat you after the last distasteful conversation you had.

This also strikes a chord with me. Years ago, in the middle of a Christmas lunch with my family, I was overcome by panic. Going to the bathroom, I did my breathing exercises, sprayed cold water on my face and hands to remind myself that I was still alive and well. I was worried that someone would ask me where I had been all that time. As soon as I was calmer, I went down to the dining room and told everyone I went to the bathroom. Nobody questioned me.

Whenever I see family or friends, I practice coping mechanisms to help me get through it; sometimes I'm even able to enjoy my time with them!

4. Conflict at the Workplace

Anger and stress can often result from disputes between co-workers. When people are depressed, they can also isolate themselves, feel guilty about letting others be disappointed, and feel guilty about getting their work done. In addition, they may feel ashamed to discuss their feelings at work because they fear retribution.

Other times, they may feel anxiety about your work, waiting for a sudden influx of customers to overwhelm them. Or perhaps they have an unkind manager who threatens to dock their pay and hours at the slightest provocation.

There are a number of symptoms that work may be a primary trigger for you, including:

- Lack of motivation to complete your daily tasks
- Having trouble concentrating
- Insomnia—which in turn also affects your productivity at work
- Loss of interest in activities you once enjoyed
- Contemplations of changing your career

We run the risk of projecting our past onto our present relationships and interactions if we fail to recognize how early negative experiences impacted us. Knowing what triggers us from the past allows us to avoid reliving past events and experiencing the emotions they evoke.

You might find this chart helpful with exploring your triggers. Using this chart, you can track the places you are when you experience a sudden increase in anxiety or depression, as well as what you experienced in those places. Over time, you'll be able to see a pattern emerging; those are your triggers.

Date	Setting	Symptoms
4 August	Brother's wedding	Pretended to be ill to avoid making a toast. Avoiding interaction with

		people, shyness, blushing, and stuttering when I speak.
23 September	Asking boss for leave	Rapid heartbeat, nausea, dizziness, dry mouth.

CHAPTER 3: COPING

The Truth About Emotions

Emotions are the result of signals sent by the brain in response to how we perceive our environment. All emotions are important and aid us in surviving and growing. Our emotions serve as guides to help us survive and flourish. We are able to experience joy when we align with aspects of our lives that bring us well-being. Anger can be an indication that there are some blocks or elements that need healing.

Whenever we feel an emotion, we are expressing a pure reaction within our bodies. It's a neutral type of energy. Perceiving emotions as inherently good or bad is unfair, because if you categorize them as negative, you risk repressing your emotions instead of expressing.

Despite the fact that our social environment often does not permit us to freely express emotions, they are meant to be neutral. The suppression of emotion is, therefore, censorship of an appropriate response. The way to free oneself from one's emotions "naturally" is to express them fully by welcoming them, and letting the discharge of their energy pass through us.

If we don't do this, and instead bottle up all emotions, that stress will feel like it's starting to crystallize, forming a dense weight within ourselves. This negatively affects our physical, mental, and emotional bodies. Emotions are neither bad or good; they serve as a survival mechanism that tells our brains how to react to situations.

In this way, emotions can be harnessed to benefit us. Our gut feelings, or the cautious voice from our subconscious, tell us about something for a reason. The presence of negative emotions can indicate that something in the environment is unstable. The sensation of fear tells us to look out and protect ourselves. The sensation of anger, on the other hand, lets us know that we have been disrespected and we need to deal with that. Joy and positive emotions should make us seek the source of our happiness and boost our wellbeing.

I hope you see that without emotions, the world and our lives would be exponentially more confusing. The idea isn't to be rid of them, but to learn how to work *with* them, not be controlled by them. If we're controlled by them, we cannot live a balanced life. If we try to smother them, we deprive ourselves of a full life. So you see there's a kind of emotional intelligence needed, so that's what we're going to discuss next.

Learning Emotional Intelligence

Research and writings by authors such as Daniel Goleman (2007) raise several interesting points concerning intelligence. We're all aware of intelligence linked to subject and skill, but many live lives not knowing about intelligence related to the self-awareness of our emotions. Emotional intelligence refers to our ability to manage, comprehend, and control our emotions. It not only helps us improve our quality of life, but it also helps us build and maintain better, more respectful, and understanding relationships with others. There are numerous facets that are involved in improving your emotional intelligence; here are a few of the most important.

Accept Your Weaknesses and Strengths

We all have our own set of qualities and shortcomings; it's what makes us human. Some people have no problem standing up for themselves, but struggle to explain how they feel, and others communicate their emotions with perfect clarity, yet struggle to support and listen to others. We must recognize that no one, present company included, is perfect. But the differences between us create a beautiful mosaic that perfection couldn't attempt. When you accept that you are a mix of bad and good, weaknesses and strengths, and then move to accept the same for the world around you, your mind will be ready to handle emotions in a right and mature way.

Express Your Feelings

This may appear to be a simple concept, yet it is likely the area where people make the most mistakes. Expressing your feelings does not imply that you should only show positive emotions, nor does it mean to give in to every random thought. It's about being able to express both good and negative emotions effectively.

The majority of relationships fail due to an inability to express ourselves in a healthy way. We improve our talents and capacities by learning to detect and communicate our emotions. Emotional intelligence realizes that emotions are truly just our bodies sending us a message as to how something affects us. This is neither good or bad. It just is. With this understanding, you can logically state your feelings (and listen to the feelings of others) without letting any reacting emotions cloud your judgement.

Confidence

This ingredient in emotional intelligence is one of the most important, yet unconscious pieces of this complicated pie. It's the opposite of passivity and avoidance, but it should still be gentle and humble. This type of confidence comes from knowing that one's emotions are valid, even if their reactions are not. This confidence enables a person to say, "I'm sorry I stormed out like that, it wasn't right. But my answer is still no. I'm not comfortable with that idea." You need to be assertive enough to take care of yourself, and kind enough to respect another person's emotions. In addition, you need to be confident enough to withstand manipulative people who may try to gaslight you, or trick you into believing that you don't understand your own emotions. If someone wants to kindly suggest another way of looking at or perceiving an event or emotion, you can take that under consideration; however, remember that you know what you feel, even if you don't understand why.

Stop Passing Judgement

We all have a tendency to evaluate others based on our ideas or moral codes. This, when communicating with others and trying to understand ourselves, is not a good thing. Now, I know this is a sensitive topic, so I want to say this clearly and gently: your actions should follow your morals. They are what you choose to do. Emotions are a *reaction*. They will exist despite morals. Now, one can choose what action *based* on an emotion, and that should follow your morals, but if one is listening to a person describe their emotions, or you're trying to understand even yourself, you should be gracious and let it all out. Otherwise, the emotions will remain bottled up until something explodes.

The people you interact with will feel different about things than you do. People differ, and it is in this diversity that the beauty of being human rests. Empathy is the most important ingredient here. Remember that you cannot judge someone unless you first put yourself in their position. Learning to remove our thinking from the dichotomy of good and evil allows us to have a more complete picture of the people around us and our feelings.

Separate Your Bad Eggs

First, we'll discuss negative coping behaviors. The key here is consistent repeated actions that are used to ignore emotions and solutions rather than work through and solve them. Individually, these are just actions that everyone does. We're talking about realizing what behaviors may be holding us back from our best lives.

As an example: if you ignore anger, you become a doormat allowing others to abuse you. When you stifle sadness, it's more likely you'll feel anxious and depressed and your body will express it in various ways. And if you refuse to feel fear, you'll become a daredevil who puts yourself in unnecessary danger.

To become aware of our emotions and feel them properly, we will have to recognize what hinders us from doing so. Unfortunately, most of the time we use negative coping techniques to ignore our emotions. The most common are avoiding, reacting, and resisting.

Avoiding

Attempting to avoid the problem involves diverting one's attention to something that will immediately make you feel better, like smoking, drinking, eating, or visiting social media, etc. Sometimes we even end up scrolling on our phones for hours. As a result, this diversion strategy leads to bad habits and even addictions in the long run. Now, ask yourself: do these help your situation? Do they help you grow into a better person? By distracting yourself from your feelings, are you helping or hindering your problems?

Reacting

We can become disconnected with what is outside ourselves when reacting to our immediate emotional states. We tend to release tension when we are angry by shouting or slamming doors. Later, however, we often will experience other negative emotions, such as embarrassment, guilt, and shame, as a result of reacting in anger. Do you consider yourself to be reactive? Consider the fact that such reactions don't better the situation or yourself; by strongly, instinctually reacting to emotions, we are distracting ourselves from healthy emotions and future growth.

Resisting

One of the most common techniques, however, is resisting. Like pressing a balloon beneath the surface of the water, we try to push our emotions down, only for them to bob up again with renewed energy. This takes incredible effort and concentration, and only makes us feel worse. The problem with this technique is, again, it doesn't last. Eventually, no matter how hard you try, the balloon must come up again, and you won't always be able to control when. Over time, you transform into something that could explode or crumble at any moment.

The problem with these strategies is that they offer no benefit, only a quick, short-term escape from unpleasant feelings. And even if you avoid negative emotions, they will still periodically return to your mind, and may even express themselves as a physical illness.

When you're put into a triggering situation that causes anxious or depressive thoughts, you likely turn to one of these negative coping behaviors. They distract you from your current situation and emotions just long enough for you to function again, but as we've mentioned, this is a temporary band-aid that causes future pain.

In order to begin the process of overcoming anxiety and depression, we need to step away from these negative coping mechanisms and replace them with positive coping mechanisms and behaviors. That is, we need to stop ignoring our emotions and instead embrace and learn from them, using positive techniques in the moment.

Positive Coping Mechanisms

I've made a distinction between coping mechanisms and coping behaviors because I believe there is a genuine difference. In the heat of the moment, I need to use a coping mechanism, a lifeline, to ground me into a place where I can act correctly. Otherwise I'll naturally use a negative coping mechanism that can cause further damage to myself and others. The consistent use of these helps me to control my emotions, which eventually leads to good coping behaviors. The mechanism is a tool to bring your emotions to a steady place; luckily, we don't need a lot of actual tools for them.

Mindful Breathing: Cool as a Cucumber

My favorite approach is to take a step back and take a few deep breaths before assessing the issue, as we mentioned before. A burst of adrenaline—your fight or flight hormone—causes that initial impulse to react. Some say that this may be beneficial for improving response time, physical strength, and other things. Unfortunately, it also reduces activity in the prefrontal cortex, which is responsible for planning and thinking in the future. Instead, you should focus on learning to manage your breathing and relax.

Why? Because your parasympathetic nervous system will restart your 'rest and digest' state. This helps you think, which helps you choose your best options. You will be calmer and more logical, and you won't be panicking waiting for the next disaster. If you react hastily (unless it's an emergency situation) you will aggravate the situation because you're not able to understand the effects or all the contributing factors. Remember the golden rule: less hurry means greater speed, especially in time-critical situations.

Using Breathing to Control Your Emotions

Breathing is a wonderful method for helping the physical body regulate the emotions that occur within us, since our emotions are also physical. It is our primary instrument for acting on our current feelings. For example, when we're angry, our heart rate and breaths per minute increase, which increases the amount of energy and oxygen in our bodies. These little alterations in the body indicate major functioning changes. But it works both ways; simply said, we can change the chemistry of our bodies (and our emotions) in just a few minutes of breathing exercises.

Each emotion has a physical manifestation and a respiratory pattern. Consider the emotion of terror: our heartbeat and our breathing both quicken, and the body adjusts to the increased alertness. Everything in our body is structured to defend itself: our muscles contract, our pupils dilate, and everything in our body is organized to defend itself. Every emotion alters the way we breathe and our whole physiological condition. Understanding gives you an advantage over your own body!

During breathing exercises, you need to engage your lower ab-dominal, middle, and thoracic muscles. The abdomen must be ex-tended outwards while breathing in via the nose, followed by the rib cage stretching to the sides, and lastly the chest moving up-wards. The diaphragm can be lowered and the rib cage can expand as a result. After that, the lungs are refilled with air. Exhale after a few minutes of holding the air in the lungs. Release the air in the opposite direction as you exhale (chest, rib cage, and abdomen). Deep breathing should be practiced numerous times a day until it becomes habitual and natural.

In daily life, mindful breathing substantially boosts our energy and vitality. When needed, you can employ this extra energy to better regulate your emotions. When used in stressful or emotional situations, this will also calm yourself enough to think rationally. They ground you into the present, rather than the ever-shifting future.

Basic Deep Breathing Recipe

Time: As much as you need, but plan for at least 10 minutes to start.

Ingredients:

- If possible, choose a quiet, uninterrupted place

Directions:

1. Sit comfortably in a chair or lie down on a couch.
2. Breathe deeply through your nose for six seconds. Focus on the air traveling through your upper chest and filling your stomach. Hold that breath for two or three seconds.
3. Keeping your lips pursed, slowly let it out.
4. Repeat 10 times. If you feel you need to, this exercise can be repeated as many times as needed; remember to listen to your body.

This slows your heart rate, making your mind and body calmer. It also brings your consciousness out of your head and into your body, as you feel the air refreshing you. You can do it alone or in a room with others; that's what makes it one of the best.

Advanced Recipe: Counting Your Breaths

Time: 10-15 minutes, this will depend on your pace.

Ingredients:

- A quiet room

Directions:

1. Ensure that you are comfortable. Lie down and close your eyes.
2. Breathe deeply; as you exhale, say the word "relax," either out loud or in your head.
3. As you breathe, relax the muscles in your face, neck, and shoulders, and count your breaths, starting at 10 and going backwards to 1.
4. When you've counted from 10 to one, you may open your eyes. If you need to, you can start at a higher number, to give you more time to calm and ground yourself.
5. Another way to do this exercise is to count the timing of your breaths. Inhale for four seconds, hold it for four seconds, and exhale for four seconds. Counting with numbers will also help you get out of the emotion and back into a more peaceful and reasonable condition.

This is my go-to ingredient for a calm mind and body, but there are several other recipes that can be both fun and beneficial.

The 1 to 5 Recipe

Time: This technique should take you no more than five minutes.

Ingredients:

- A quiet place

Directions:

1. Describe one thing that you can taste. If you have snacks in your bags, grab one. If you don't have candy, notice any tastes in your mouth. Think about the last time you drank water and felt hydrated, or picture your favorite meal.
2. Name two different smells. You can name the scent of

your perfume, the soap in the kitchen, the smell of rain if it is pouring outside. Try to picture what it would smell like right now.

3. Touch three objects, like a pencil in front of you, a stress ball, or lipgloss. Think about the texture, weight of these objects and their uses. Do they feel warm or cool? Are they in good condition?

4. Pay attention to four different sounds. You might be surprised on where they came from and how different they are from one another. Pay attention to the birds chirping, the music in the background, and footsteps of someone walking nearby.

5. Take a look at five different objects. For a short while, reflect on each. What makes them different from each other, the color, size, and function of each item. It could be the same objects that you used in step three.

Exercises like these are designed to engage your other senses and alleviate overthinking about your current situation. They make you mindful of your moment, and help ground you into your current reality, rather than the spiral of your negative thoughts. This helps you make good decisions because you will become focused on what is actually happening rather than every possible future outcome. As a result, you're able to make a decision that best fits your reality, rather than an imaginary future event.

But if you feel that you're in an area that doesn't have a lot of sensory happenings for you to focus on, you can try this next mindfulness exercise.

Raisins and Mindfulness

Time: Five minutes should be enough to complete this mindfulness exercise.

Ingredients:

- Raisin (you can use a dried fruit or any other food that has an interesting shape).

Directions:

This is a great exercise to start practicing mindfulness since it can be attempted by anyone with any kind of food.

1. Grab a raisin or any small-sized food. Imagine as though this is the very first time you are seeing this raisin. This exercise is almost meant to engage your five senses.
2. Look at how small the raisin is! Feel its texture, and how light it is in your hand. Move the raisin and see how the surface responds to the motion. Does it smell like anything? What does it taste like?

The purpose of focusing on the raisin is to make you aware of what you are doing right now. Many of us are accustomed to raisin snacks and fail to take the trouble to examine them. Whether we use them to bake or snack, how many of us really take the time to pay attention to the foods that we use.

Look for the Solution

Now that you're calm, you can find the most effective answer to the situation at hand. It's harmful and even foolish to try to make important decisions while you're feeling any strong emotion, much less anxious or depressed. For instance, if you're feeling anxious and are called to make a decision, you'll end up holding onto familiar things, but only out of fear. You might choose to keep a job you dislike, or choose not to start a hobby; this fear has officially affected your behavior and actions. As long as your fear controls you, your life and behavior will forever remain the same.

The opposite is also true: if you learn to become aware of how fear is affecting you, and then learn how to calm yourself when you feel yourself spiraling, you will be able to change your behavior. As a result, you will learn how to choose your actions not based on emotions, even if feelings of fear are occasionally felt. This is true for every emotion, which is why it's so very important to learn how to embrace your feelings without being controlled by them.

Once you've carefully evaluated your alternatives and calculated the best course of action, the next step is to simply act. Take positive and decisive action, even if you are unsure. Accepting the potential that things may go wrong on your call is a necessary part of this process. The only other option is to stay stuck in the negative situation forever. You have to be able and willing to go out on a limb and confront whatever storm may arise.

Peace of Mind

All of us long for serenity through life's tumult and diversions. We want to get away from it all or seize control to bring order out of chaos. We want to be calm and peaceful. However, unless we move to the mountains and live in a monastery, this type of search for removing turmoil and tension is usually not achievable. So, what are your options? The solution is to achieve serenity and peace in the middle of the troubles. Meditation is one method for finding tranquility.

You may feel this today, even on your commute or at work, if you find the time and space to sit quietly for a minute or two. Sit in a position that makes you feel at ease. First, perform a body scan. What sensations do you have? Is your posture calm and straight? Then examine your respiration. Is your breathing calm? For a few moments, focus your attention on your breathing. Next, expand your awareness to include the entire space, including yourself. Maintain awareness of your surroundings while keeping your eyes open.

You become aware of all feelings without assigning labels to them. Do not pass judgment on anything, and do not become fixated on anything in particular; simply observe. If your mind begins to wander in thought throughout any of these processes, pay attention to it (without judgment). Then, slowly bring your attention back to the current moment or your breathing. If you can rest in this observation condition, you can return to it when you wander. Try it for a minute to see if you can relax. Recognize that you do not have to be involved in everything that comes to mind. You can work in such a way that you feel as if you are watching a movie or a play in which you are an actor. What I've discovered is that when you can do it, it's incredibly peaceful.

This is the sensation you can experience if you remain in a state of observation with an open mind and a sense of being linked to everything. Stay in that calm for as long as you can or want to. If you can get a glimpse of this sense of quiet or peace in the preceding meditation, you can return to it at any time. When you're feeling stressed, pause to regain your sense of calm. During an argument or when stuck in traffic, you can find peace by meditating and returning to this state of quiet.

Keep in mind that you can access it at any time of day. When you notice an emotion that has generated a stress response, that you are agitated, and that you have a sense of anxiety, return to that point of tranquility. It only takes a few minutes. Simply by being a part of everything around you, you may let go of your sense of self. Reestablish contact with your inner quiet. Find love and compassion for all of the aspects that are suffering. Then you can continue to accomplish what you need to do at this time by carrying out your daily chores while maintaining a sense of calm during the commotion. Be in touch with the infinite all around you, and feel at ease while you take action. There is no need to flee the pandemonium. It's simply a movement that you must learn to live with! Every adversity is an opportunity for personal development and emotional mastery.

CHAPTER 4: THE ICING ON THE CAKE

Every day we are exposed to a wide variety of things that may affect our emotions. Our lifestyles, the people we associate with, achievements and objectives, weather conditions, and our state of mind are just some of the things that have an impact (positive or negative) on us. If you don't know how to find the good, you're stuck in a pattern of negative behavior and thoughts, and then you have a bad day, then you might find yourself spiraling. The last thing you want is for this emotion to become overpowering.

But when you consistently use healthy coping mechanisms to calm your emotions and put yourself back in charge of your decisions, you will eventually see overwhelmingly positive life changes. When you're calm, you're able to make better life decisions, which make your life more positive, leading to less consistently negative situations. As you learn this, you may see or choose to begin some of the following positive coping behaviors.

You Are What You Eat

I'm sure you've heard how highly it is recommended that you include some regular exercise and a healthy diet in your lifestyle. When you stop coping by distracting yourself with food, you're able to make better choices. By feeding yourself good foods and only indulging occasionally, you're ensuring that your physical body is running at 100%. When your body feels better, your mind feels better. You can even engage the mind in this process by deciding to cook your own food; this is healthy learning, and a distraction from negative thoughts.

Quality Sleep

If you do not get good sleep after having a busy day or after an activity, it is likely that your mind or body will be exhausted, which can lead to depression. Maybe one of your negative coping mechanisms is staying awake into the wee hours of the morning, scrolling on your phone. But this forces your mind to take on more than it can physically handle, therefore causing long-term dizziness and fatigue. A good night's sleep can also help with a variety of other elements of our health. Because fatigue raises adrenaline levels, it makes you more prone to stress. Sleep is essential for optimal performance and emotional equilibrium. For your mind to rest adequately, most physicians recommend at least 6-8 hours of sleep a day. When you stop coping by staying up late, you automatically get more hours of rest. As a result, you'll be able to better manage your stress.

Sanity, Prioritized

Last but not least, as the quality of your life improves based on your positive coping mechanisms, you'll learn this one important thing: there is enough time in a day for everything.

Does all of this mean that your life will be peaceful and trigger free? Unfortunately, no. The world can be beautiful and chaotic, like a kaleidoscope. And sometimes our brains 'go off' in certain situations that cause us to be led by our feelings instead of logic. This often results in regrettable behavior. But can it be avoided? Imagine being able to control 100% of our emotions, reactions, and thoughts; regardless of the situation, you could listen to and respect yourself, and therefore be in harmony with yourself and others. That's the whole goal! But in order to live in harmony, you must first know yourself, and what situations trigger an overly emotional response.

You will keep attracting the same situations and repeating the same attitudes and behavior patterns (which keep feeding your wounds) if you do not take the time to heal them. As you heal your wounds, your emotions become less powerful, which gives you more control over your behavior; ultimately, healing these wounds is the key to growing and evolving. But in order to do that, there are a few things you need to remember:

First: Self-commitment is necessary for healing to occur. During the healing process, your biggest obligation <u>must</u> be yourself; you will not have success if healing others is your focus in this time. That can come later.

Second: Be aware that these wounds are part of who you are, and that's ok; in fact, they are the key to open the door to restoration. A person's emotional pain, whether conscious or unconscious, is completely normal and human. Humans are imperfect.

Third: Pay attention to your emotions, your feelings, and your reactions; you must choose to do this, because action is key. Thinking about maybe healing yourself doesn't do you any good. During this process remember this: when it comes to knowing what is right and good for you, your heart knows.

Fourth: Don't place too much importance on the negative experiences you've had in the past. Learning from those lessons is the right decision; living the rest of your life staying in shock of it isn't. Be at peace with your conscious and unconscious feelings about the past. Get a fresh perspective on your experience by taking a step back; then you can adapt your experience to your future. Rather than let the wound fester, shut the door to the past. Healing allows you to build a better future for yourself.

Decisive Positive Action

Weir (2011) suggests that depression is at least partly the result of our day-to-day lifestyle. Although our lifestyles are made up of innumerable things, some of the most obvious are our eating habits, our way of exercising, the way we relate to people, and our living arrangements. As we improve our lifestyles, we see incredibly positive changes to our physical, mental, and emotional bodies.

Along with using positive coping mechanisms and their natural results, we must also take decisive action to better ourselves and avoid triggers. I've come up with six strategies to avoid negative spirals; I hope that you keep these essential things in mind, so you can be happy and even see a ray of hope in whatever scenario you find yourself in.

1. Surround yourself with genuine people. Hanging out with positive individuals assists you in maintaining your good attitude. You can join a gym and get to know a group of people, or if you are someone who likes to take coffee breaks at a different time from everyone, you can share coffee breaks with your colleagues. To meet people from different backgrounds, you can also take painting or poetry classes. Negative individuals should be avoided since their negativity will rub off on you. They will turn you back into a cynic after you have tried to attain optimism.

2. Do not let work issues interfere with your family life. Many people make the common mistake of dragging issues from their career lives to their homes, which in turn causes them more grief and makes the situation worse. Thus, you must draw a line. Leave all work-related issues at work, and spend quality time with your family. Relax as much as possible without being con-

cerned about what tomorrow may bring. No job is worth your and your family's sanity.

3. Remind yourself of the things for which you are thankful. We need to think about the good things in our lives when we are in a bad circumstance, to remind ourselves of all the good we have to look forward to. You should express appreciation and positive sentiments. Develop a habit of focusing on the positive aspects of your life rather than the negative aspects. It's also a good idea to keep a daily record of all the positive things you've accomplished and seen, for you to look back on during hard times. Even in the face of adversity, appreciating what you are grateful for will help you cultivate a grateful heart and mind.

4. Take responsibility for your errors. Accept responsibility if you make a mistake, and reward yourself if you accomplish anything nice. Do not place blame on others for things that are your fault. This just attracts bad energy to you by seeing the mistake as a huge, negatively emotional thing to be avoided. We need to learn from our mistakes! Accept the circumstances as they are, own your mistake, learn from it, and go on with your life. Robert Kiyosaki said, "Don't waste a good mistake, learn from it." He wanted to encourage people to live as regret-free as possible. The sentiment is supported by Albert Einstein, who expressed that if you don't make mistakes, you won't try anything new. In other words, if you didn't fail, how could you tell if you weren't prepared? When you don't get the job, how else would you find out that you needed to keep growing your skillset?

5. Keep your life free of drama. Drama is an unwelcome and unpleasant hindrance to your mental health. Don't entertain dramatic individuals, and try to avoid the rumor mill; this is just a part of avoiding drama. They don't

serve a purpose, except to propagate negativity.

6. Be considerate of others. This helps you to appreciate the small kindnesses of life, and will reinforce your self-confidence in your own goodness.

Write Down Your Thoughts

A journal is a place where we may write down all of our ideas, worries, and feelings that are taking up space in our minds. To clear their minds, most individuals write down their worries in it before going to bed. This helps you process events and emotions without stewing on them. You can also reflect on your day and write in your journal about what you loved doing or what you are grateful for. This daily activity can assist you in focusing on the positive aspects of your life while removing the negative thoughts from your head. The act of writing in a journal can be incredibly therapeutic and beneficial in lowering anxiety and tension.

In assessing your negative thinking, you may find that some of the things you fear rarely occur, or if they do, they're not as bad as you thought they would be. Writing your anxious thoughts down can enable you to evaluate them and identify more realistic ways to approach them.

Cue the Music

You might be astonished to learn that there are over 7000 different languages spoken throughout the world. And, while most of us will only learn a few of them in our lives, music is unquestionably the one universal language of our world. We all have an emotional response to different chords and melodies, regardless of our culture or background, and there is now strong scientific evidence supporting the premise that music can play a role in the enhancement of mental health.

Music can help lower anxiety and tension by up to 65 percent, as well as boost your mood and prevent depression (Wheeler, 2017). As an added benefit, it can also boost blood flow, lower stress-related chemicals such as cortisol, and ease pain. Listening to music before surgery can even boost post-operative outcomes.

How can music be so beneficial? Music appears to preferentially activate neurochemical systems and brain regions linked with positive mood, emotion management, attention, and memory, promoting favorable changes. Music can also cause the release of dopamine, a hormone that makes people feel good, as well as endorphins, which are hormones that can generate positive moods and relieve pain. Music therapy is not a cure for depression, but it can improve mood, promote self-expression, and encourage connection.

If you want to utilize music to de-stress, motivate yourself, or otherwise change your mental or emotional condition. You most likely already have a collection of music that you know will have the desired effect. Dive right in! Just keep distractions to a minimum. No one can truly multitask. While listening to motivating music can make your work out harder or for longer periods, listening to soothing music while reading through your news or social feeds will not help you unwind.

Consider music therapy, a specialty that focuses on utilizing music to enhance patient outcomes, to build an even deeper link between music and your health. Music therapy begins with a person who wants to feel more whole or optimistic but is unaware that music can assist. One type of music therapy is guided imagery in music (Cohen, 2018). A skilled therapist there assists a person in discovering her strengths or obstacles by listening to music chosen by the patient. Music can create a sense of therapist-patient attunement. Sharing music makes the patient feel as if the therapist "truly understands me."

Other types of music therapy may include singing or instrument playing. The way we compose music can reveal information about ourselves that a therapist can use to help us. Someone may play a drum in only one tempo or dynamic, which may indicate their inability to be adaptable in other aspects of their life. Music allows us to bypass our reasoning half and connect with our emotional side, which we frequently keep hidden. When individuals are in distress, there is generally a method that music may help.

Choose a Physical Lifestyle

Physical activity has also been shown to improve mental health and emotional balance. Exercise helps to channel the adrenaline generated into the body during times of stress. Many people go to the gym to relieve stress and enhance their overall health. Physical activity also releases serotonin and endorphins, which contribute to a positive mood. Cardio is fantastic, but even a low-intensity activity like strolling can have a significant impact on your mood. Exercise improves several aspects of health by increasing endorphin levels. Gotlin (2020) explains that endorphins are natural chemicals that are released when we do anything that requires a burst of energy. They are the stuff that makes us perform, makes us move. The release of endorphins contributes to the exhilaration frequently referred to as a runner's high.

Exercise improves your heart function, allowing you to work out longer throughout the day. When it's easier to do daily tasks, you'll have more energy and won't be as fatigued when work is through. The American Heart Association (2010) recommends at least 30 minutes of moderate-intensity aerobic activity five days a week for general cardiovascular health. Aim for 150 minutes of moderate to vigorous-intensity aerobic activity three to four times per week to decrease cholesterol and blood pressure.

When beginning a new workout routine, be patient. Most inactive persons need four to eight weeks to feel coordinated and in good enough shape to exercise comfortably. Find ways to exercise that are joyful or fun. Classes and group activities are popular among extroverts. Introverted people often prefer to do things alone. Instead of focusing on ideal workouts, set tiny daily goals and strive for everyday consistency. It's better to go for a 20-minute walk every day than to save a three-hour fitness marathon for the weekend.

Life Redesigned

Eventually, the practice of positive coping mechanisms and behaviors will lead you to a place where you can just relax, even in chaotic situations. Stress is frequently accompanied by a sense of powerlessness and loss of control. Finding a means to practice letting go of situations you don't have control over can be beneficial, but it isn't always possible. You might not be able to let go of work deadlines, for example. Acceptance is the only power you have in these situations. Accept that you have no control over the circumstance while simultaneously acknowledging that tension will not change it. Then you have power over how you react to the event. You'll acquire confidence in your capacity to manage obstacles and have a positive attitude as a result of doing so. You may even be able to laugh at the immense tasks before you, knowing that you'll be able to come out well on the other side.

Speaking of laughter, something I want you to do is to look for the humor in the world around you. Laughter is always beneficial to your body; it releases endorphins just like during physical exertion. Laughter also helps to alleviate anxiety. A simple smile might also have a positive impact on your health. It can elicit pleasant emotions in a difficult environment, even if it is forced. Make an effort to include more joy and play in your life. Children are excellent at teaching us how to play, so spending more time with them might not be a terrible idea.

CHAPTER 5: SELF CARE
AND BOUNDARIES

The World Health Organization (2021) defines self-care as anything an individual can do to protect themselves from getting ill or to cope with sickness without the assistance of a medical professional. A sense of self care includes everything you need to do to stay healthy, like staying hygienic, eating right, and getting medical attention when you need it. It's all the steps a person can take in order to manage stress in their lives, to take care of their wellbeing and health at the same time.

People with codependency have a tough time setting boundaries and taking care of themselves. Perhaps as a child, you were taught that it is your responsibility to take care of others. When you are responsible for others, you often have to provide for them at the expense of yourself. Probably, you inherited this need to take care of others from your childhood as well. There is a large percentage of codependent people who were neglected children meaning that their parents and siblings were left to care for them from an early age. The result is that there is hardly any energy, money, or time left to take care of oneself.

Maybe there didn't seem to be any role models around you who guided you towards healthy boundaries and self-care. Due to the lack of instruction on how to set boundaries and take good care of ourselves, most of us struggle with learning how to practice good self care. The result is the erroneous belief that self-care and boundaries are selfish is ingrained in our minds.

As a child, did you ever get told to suck it up, to stop crying, or to stop being too sensitive? Many people have memories of being told that they're selfish or disrespectful when they set aside time to take care of themselves, or say no for any reason. Having feelings that are criticized, unimportant, or unacceptable as a child can cause codependents to believe that their needs and feelings don't matter. As a result, they learn to push their feelings aside and pretend that they don't need anything.

But, according to this train of thought, how can you take care of others if you are falling apart? You can't! So for the sake of others, you need to practice self-care and boundaries so you can be your best.

Furthermore, aren't you "others" to other people? That is, aren't you a person that another person would consider helping, which makes you worthy of the same kindness you offer others? You are! So because you are a person deserving kindness, you must practice self care and boundaries so you can be your best. So let's begin by discussing how to practice self care to keep your body and mind in tip-top condition.

Maintaining Good Sleep Hygiene

It is important that you have healthy habits that make it easier for you to fall asleep and wake up feeling refreshed. The cause of sleep disorders such as insomnia can often be traced to bad habits that have grown stronger over time.

Don't Ignore Your Body Clock

Getting up at the same time every morning is the best way to be successful. The more you follow this strict routine, the sooner your body clock will be able to be set so that you'll be able to fall asleep at the same time every night.

- Tiredness is not to be taken lightly. Your body will tell you when it is time to go to sleep, so listen to it.
- If you are not feeling tired, you shouldn't go to bed. This only reinforces bad habits, such as staying awake all night.
- Don't forget to get enough sunshine in the mornings. Your body clock is set to wake up as early as possible in the morn-

ings when you are exposed to light.

Key Ingredients for a Better Sleep Environment

In order to sleep better, you should make sure that your bedroom has a relaxing and comfortable atmosphere.

- Getting a comfortable mattress that is neither too hard nor too soft is important.
- If the room is at an uncomfortable temperature, make sure that the thermostat is set properly.
- It is very important to ensure that the room is adequately dark.
- A pair of earplugs would be useful if you are not able to control noise, e.g. your pet barking or your neighbor being loud.
- Sleeping and intimacy are the only things you should do in your bedroom. In the event that you use your bedroom, for example, as a second lounge room—to watch television or talk on the phone with friends—then your brain will build a mental association that it is an area where activity is being performed.

Going Green: Time Outdoors

Being social in nature is part of who we are as humans. We live in a society in which we are increasingly isolating ourselves from social interaction. Many people do not think about the fact that staying inside has other negative consequences that are often not realized. In reality, there are countless benefits to being outdoors and in nature that you will not be able to gain when you are locked inside your house. Nature is a vital part of your health and well-being, so it's important to ensure you spend plenty of time outdoors.

There are several benefits for your mind and body that you cannot gain from being inside during the winter months. Such benefits include exposure to direct sunlight and fresh air. Vanbuskirk

(2020) believes that exposure to natural sunlight can improve a person's mood as well as self-esteem as a whole. On bright, sunny days, the brain releases more serotonin than it does on a cold day, regardless of whether the temperature is cold or warm. The serotonin your body produces helps stabilize your mood and also reduces depression and anxiety symptoms.

You can spend your time outdoors in a number of different ways. When we exercise we release endorphins; these are hormones that make our bodies naturally feel good and good about ourselves. Additionally, the act of exercising can also lead to a calmer state of mind as well as help to burn off excess energy that may be the cause of stress and anxiety. Here are a few of my favorite activities:

- Walk or run for a few minutes
- Outdoor yoga or meditation
- Biking or hiking along a trail
- Start creating a flower or vegetable garden
- Swimming
- Camping
- Getting friends or family together for a picnic

Keeping your mind fit and healthy can be achieved by participating in outdoor activities. Despite the fact that it is nice to have a comfortable home, the air inside is not quite as healthy as the air outside. Even just taking a walk in nature for 20-30 minutes every day will help you feel better.

Finding a Hobby

If you are experiencing abnormal levels of anxiety or stress, it is a good idea to take up a hobby. While entertaining you, it can also take your mind off any feelings or thoughts that you may be experiencing that might be negative at the time. The enjoyment of a leisure activity is an excellent way to soothe an overactive mind while alleviating anxiety and lowering panic symptoms. The only way for you to discover what works for you is through trial and error, what is right for your friend might not be right for you, so be patient and try a few different things until you discover what is right for you.

Tap Into Your Creative Brain

You can use drawing, painting, card making, candle making, and scrapbooking as examples of manual tasks that can provide you with an opportunity to express yourself and create something of your own at the same time. You may wish to add to your story, write a poem, write a letter, or keep a journal to express emotions that have built up over time. Cooking can also be a fascinating hobby, and there is the added benefit of getting a mouth-watering meal afterward. There is nothing wrong with eating a dish that does not have to be extravagant like something you might find in the MasterChef competition, but it is fun to check out new recipes, taste new foods, and learn about different kinds of flavor.

Find a Pet Friend

Stress can be reduced by interacting with animals. If you play with and stroke an animal, you will increase your levels of the stress-reducer oxytocin and lessen your levels of the stress-stimulating hormone cortisol due to the reduction of your stress-reducing hormones (Blinder, 2013). As a result, we feel better naturally. Perhaps you could be of assistance at a local rescue center if you are not able to adopt a pet personally.

Take a Picture and Smile

We are no longer reliant upon expensive cameras to pursue this hobby as it is not a difficult one. There are many mobile phones that take good pictures. Photographing the nature of the sea as part of therapy is highly recommended. By going out and taking pictures for a specific purpose, you will be surprised by the way you view the world around you. While we all have a variety of interests, switching your life up a little bit and trying something new can really make a difference.

Even Dough Needs to Rest

People sometimes frown upon self-care, setting boundaries, and prioritizing their own needs, which in fact are vital to their well-being. The codependent person often sacrifices their own needs in order to keep others happy or keep conflict to a minimum, which is why they can have problems dealing with these struggles. In order to maintain your personal safety and to live in alignment with your values, you need to learn how to let go of guilt and to recognize that asking for what you need and setting boundaries is essential to keeping you safe.

Self-care is anything you do to maintain a fit, healthy, and happy mind, body, and emotions. As a result, we achieve better health, fulfillment, and well-being on all levels of our lives. Lawyer (2020) suggests that self-care enhances resilience, increases lifespan, and improves depression coping skills. Self-care begins with setting and adhering to clear and defined boundaries. By acknowledging your needs and requesting assistance from others, you are taking action.

When you don't set boundaries, you run the risk of losing yourself. You don't know what you feel, what you are interested in, or what you want. Our decision-making is often left to someone else. There are times when we give and give to the point where we don't receive anything in return. It also makes us vulnerable to being used and manipulated by others, because we do not set limits on how we allow others to treat us.

Our intellect tells us that we must take care of ourselves first before we can try to take care of others. What is it that makes us feel guilty when we take care of ourselves? And why is it so difficult for us to consistently practice self-care? Do you feel like your current self-care practices are meeting your needs, or can they be improved?

Sadly, our boundaries are not as evident as a fence or a huge "no trespassing" sign. I would describe them as invisible bubbles. Regardless of the difficulties involved in setting and communicating personal boundaries, they are necessary for our physical and psychological health. By setting boundaries to one's space, body, and emotions, boundaries confer a sense of control. Everybody has limits, and boundaries communicate these limits.

Instincts can help you recognize when someone is violating your boundaries or when one needs to be set. If you're not sure where you should draw the line, listen to your body; your heart rate, sweating, tightness in your chest, stomach, throat. Your fists might clench when you lend out that new coat to your roommate, for example. Sometimes you hold your breath when relatives ask about your dating life.

There can be some confusion surrounding the word "boundary." The meaning conveys that you should keep yourself separate. Nevertheless, boundaries are essential for navigating intimate and professional relationships, as they provide healthy rules.

Make your safety and comfort the primary focus of your attention. It's very common for people to obstruct setting and enforcing boundaries due to their feelings of guilt or fear of a negative reaction. Boundaries are not just about building healthy relationships with others, but about boosting your self-esteem and your self-love, too!

Having lived a life taking care of others before taking care of myself-being unhealthy and drained all the time I know this for sure: Until you take care of yourself, you will not be able to be the beacon you are meant to be.

Stress or pressure that causes us to no longer react to love is a sign that something is wrong. There is a need for balance. We should remember self-care when we let anything other than love come out of us. Giving comes naturally to many of us. Empaths, like me, allow the energy of others to drastically influence their lives. It is not uncommon for you to feel drained. Unempowered empaths are emotionally depleted, physically worn out, and spiritually depleted.

Are there ever times when you feel guilty taking care of yourself? Most women feel guilty and selfish about taking care of themselves, even those who do the inner work. As long as we care for ourselves and don't feel guilty about it, we will be more rested, calm, and loving. The "juice" that will emerge from us when we are squeezed will contain the qualities of love and centeredness. You are not selfish by caring for yourself. You have a sacred responsibility to take care of yourself.

You can analyze and improve your self-care practices more easily if you permit yourself to love yourself first.

Boundaries: The Perfect Way for Saying No

While you are beginning the process of recovering from co-dependency, I recommend you take a moment to become conscious of your thoughts and behaviors—challenging yourself to think about things differently and taking small steps to act in ways that reflect your growing self-respect and self-understanding. Keep in mind that boundaries are an important part of self-care. When you consider that everyone has needs, it's less likely for you to feel guilty when you consider that taking care of yourself is a good thing to do. Taking care of your own needs is nothing to be ashamed of!

Family and Relationships

Relationships, especially healthy ones, should be mutually supportive and should yield benefits for both parties involved. In life, we all go through times when we need a little bit more support than usual. In the long run, a relationship that requires too much of us or makes us feel bad at the end is unhealthy. In order to protect yourself, it is important to set boundaries. If you don't want to stay in toxic relationships, you need to figure out a way to break yourself off from them. Don't waste your time, energy, or love on negative relationships, the same applies to family relations.

Here are some simple ideas that will help you set some boundaries:

1. Knocking before entering a room
2. Designating areas or times to give each other space
3. Agreeing to leave phones out of mealtimes

In the world of relationships, boundaries represent a space or separation between two people. If you set up a physical barrier between you and someone, such as stepping away or closing a door, you literally create more distance between you and them. A psychological boundary helps you make room for your own feelings, needs, beliefs, or interests from other people's feelings, needs, beliefs, and interests.

It is also beneficial for those around you when you establish boundaries and exercise self-care. When your needs and expectations are clearly communicated and understood by others, things run more smoothly and you feel respected when your expectations and needs are clearly communicated. Taking care of yourself is also important as it will keep you healthier and happier in the long run. In the long run, you will be more motivated to accomplish daily tasks, will harbor less resentment towards others, and will have more patience for personal problems.

Time is Everything

One thing that we can never get back is time. You can manage your time wisely if you set boundaries regarding the activities you choose to do with your free time. Decide to prioritize free time and learn to say no to things that do not align with your values or things that you don't want to do. It is a good thing to be firm in the fact that you won't allow yourself to feel pulled in several directions at the same time.

Keeping a time boundary that allows you to protect your time is another important aspect to consider. An example of time boundaries that could be implemented includes turning off screen notifications or not answering your phone after a certain time in the evening. unless in an emergency. When you reduce the amount of access that people have to you, you will reduce the feelings of anxiety that come with feeling like you are needed during a crisis or difficult time. In some cases, we can feel unable to even engage in a simple conversation for fear of being overwhelmed.

Money Matters

Creating boundaries around money management will help you save more, invest better, stop spending unnecessary money, and beat temptation. Set up better systems to manage, spend, and save your money once you decide what you want from it. Consider setting money boundaries by, for example, not using credit cards or putting aside a percentage of your monthly income as soon as you get paid.

Even though it can be intimidating to say, "No," it's a complete statement. It's not necessary to always feel the need to justify your decisions. Boundary setting sometimes doesn't require assertiveness, but rather a tolerance for being uncomfortable. You can say no without having to explain yourself or without burdening the person with emotional labor. You are free to decline requests for your number or to dance. A coworker can also ask you to cover their shift, but you can refuse with no need for an explanation.

Develop Self-Awareness

Your gut will tell you what to do! A big part of creating boundaries is prioritizing your comfort so you can be present with others and feel safe, but to do that, you have to acknowledge and honor your feelings. Are there any things that make you feel safe? Is there anything that makes you uncomfortable? You may find that your boundaries change as you grow; allow this to happen and hold space for yourself to recognize and acknowledge these feelings.

Be Honest About Your Limits

Get in touch with your feelings and determine what you need physically, emotionally, and mentally so that you can identify your limits and more effectively communicate them. This can be accomplished using a boundary circle. You can do this by drawing a circle on a piece of paper. Create a list of everything you need to feel seen, heard, supported, and safe. Anything actively in conflict or distracting from that should be written outside the circle. Keeping your boundaries consistent is important. There are times when we need to communicate with others if they cross our boundaries. We can't expect other people to know what we're feeling at any given time.

Keep It Simple, Direct, and Clear

Be as clear and calm as possible when you are setting and enforcing boundaries. It's okay to set boundaries without justifying, defending, or apologizing for them. The tone or manner of enforcing your boundaries can always be adjusted if desired. Depending on where you are emotionally on a given day, your level of assertiveness is determined by the relationship you have with the other person, the circumstances, and even the relationship you are in with the other person. For those of you who are nervous or sensitive about certain boundaries, you can prepare your lines in advance to make sure those lines are respected.

Setting boundaries can make you feel anxious or uncomfortable, so start small. No one should feel guilty for saying no, but it takes practice! In a situation where you are not comfortable doing a favor for someone, you can offer some kind of tool that will help or another person who can help.

Know Thyself

"The more you know yourself, the more patience you have for what you see in others." - Erik Erikson

A crucial part of healing yourself is knowing who you are. It's impossible to avoid a disaster if you run around life not knowing what you stand for or what you won't stand for. Small-town girls with big dreams often find themselves compromising themselves and miserable, which is often the case when they move to the big city. You may also think about an unhappy doctor whose parents made him become the first doctor in their family because they wanted him to be one. Suppose he dates a girl he can't stand just because his mother loves her? There are many similarities between these three instances. They have the problem that is explained by the old saying, "We will take any road if we don't know where we're going." If we don't stand for anything, we will fall for anything.

It is easy for almost anyone to push us into a decision we will regret for the rest of our lives if we don't understand ourselves, this includes our hopes, dreams, and aspirations. Being forced to live with the consequences of a choice you regret every day will be one of the hardest things you've ever had to do. Many people are bitter and unkind because they are living with the burden of their decisions. This is not how you should approach life. The key to unlocking our true potential lies in understanding who we are and why we act the way we do. Unless you know what your best self looks like, you cannot become that person.

Choosing a career you enjoy is much more likely if you understand who you are. When you pursue a career that you love, it is quite easy to be passionately driven to succeed. Also, when you're at the top of your game, you'll seek out partners and friends who make you happy and will thus bring the best out of you. You will understand their perspective, and they may very well think as you do too. A person like this will not mock your achievements or laugh at your dreams. You will be kinder, happier, and might I even say, more successful when you are surrounded by loving, supportive people.

A person with an in-depth understanding of themselves is usually more decisive and optimistic in their life decisions. These people make good life choices because they have full control over their lives. Where others see a setback, they see an opportunity. Being productive is also easier when you enjoy what you're doing. You will also have a competitive edge and will no longer be dependent on others for motivation if you enjoy your career. Having a sense of accomplishment keeps you motivated. Although these circumstances may seem ideal, in which a person's decisions are not dictated by family pressures, where they cannot pressure the other to make a particular decision. But believe me, understanding and knowing yourself will lead to opportunities you would have never experienced otherwise.

Know Thy Limits

"A great man is always willing to be little."

- Ralph Waldo Emerson

Your strengths and weaknesses are (no surprise here) an important part of yourself. Many of the errors we make and the challenges we face may have been avoided entirely if we were better informed about our limitations. Consider a zealous weightlifter who attempts to lift too much, too quickly. What do you think is going to happen? Any logical person can see that the weightlifter is going to injure himself.

Some may argue that this depiction encourages us to set limits for ourselves and that if we do, we will never realize our true potential. "If you put your mind to it, there are no limits to what you can accomplish, and you never know how strong you are until you try!" But when working to achieve your goals , you must make sure that logic and reason win. If you've never lifted more than 20 pounds before, starting with 20 pounds today would be a better option than trying to start with 50. There's nothing wrong with dreaming big, but I recommend beginning small and working your way up, for the safety and health of your mind and body

This will not only assist you in avoiding unreasonable expectations, but it will also assist you in establishing realistic periods for achieving your objectives. When people reach a certain age and have not accomplished a given goal, they grow frustrated. Take, for example, the difference between Mark Zuckerberg and Colonel Sanders. Colonel Sanders did not become the founder of Kentucky Fried Chicken until he was eighty years old. Mark Zuckerberg built his Facebook empire in his early twenties. Both individuals are considered to be extremely successful, yet their prosperity came at vastly different ages and life stages. Maybe it's just not the appropriate time for you, or maybe you're in the wrong industry.

Choosing a career in which you are passionate will help you stay motivated and achieve success. Both of these men's lives provide witness to this viewpoint. Their success sprang from a strong desire to do what they enjoyed. A modest outlook on life will also prevent you from comparing your accomplishments to those of others. Some people can hit the ball out of the park right away, while others must work their way up the ladder.

Some people marry straight after graduation, while others must wait a few years and kiss a few frogs before finding the ideal partner. In reality, on their journey to success, both Mark Zuckerberg and Colonel Sanders faced numerous disappointments. You will as well. Expect nothing different from your life. Whatever you want to do, you'll have to work harder than you've ever worked before, and you may have to wait longer than you anticipated. The attractive attribute of modesty goes far beyond achieving achievement. This trait will assist you in not biting off more than you can chew.

You don't have to agree to everything that people ask of you. Both personally and professionally, you should maintain a balance between the two. If you want to impress your boss, don't agree to ridiculous deadlines unless you're certain you'll be able to accomplish the assignment. If you've been given an assignment and are unclear how to do it, don't be hesitant to seek assistance. If you have a full-time job and a family to support, don't overextend yourself at your child's school. Know what you're capable of! This is true in terms of your time, energy, emotions, and abilities. Modesty and honesty go hand in hand, and the next chapter will describe how you can use this ability to cure yourself and enhance your life.

Embrace Honesty

*"Honesty is the fastest way to prevent a mistake
from turning into a failure."*

- James Altucher

When you look for synonyms for the word honesty, you'll discover honor, sincerity, fairness, integrity, uprightness, virtue, and truthfulness. Being truthful entails more than simply avoiding lying in a crisis. Being truthful necessitates being morally upright in all aspects of life. To put it another way, we will endeavor to be honest in all we do and earn the trust of people around us by our actions. However, honesty is a difficult concept to grasp. It's difficult to enumerate all of the places where we must be truthful. If you're unclear if an act is honest or not, consider whether you'll have to hide it or trick someone into believing you did something else. You're probably not being honest if you have to hide or cover your traces after doing or saying anything.

The advantages of being truthful far surpass any difficulties you may encounter as a result of this training. Consider the relief of not having to second-guess your every step or continuously look over your shoulder for fear of being discovered. Imagine not waking up with a heavy sense of guilt as a result of your activities. And don't be misled into believing that your honesty will help no one. It's extremely simple to be drawn to and appreciate someone truthful. When looking for new hires or contemplating a promotion within their company, most employers consider honesty to be of the highest significance. Along with the benefits of honesty, consider the effects of dishonesty:

- Your reputation is damaged
- A sense of anger and guilt can lead to doubting your decision abilities
- Sleep deprivation and restlessness
- Loss of integrity in your relationship with others
- Loss of money and opportunities to do business with others
- Damaged self-respect and reliability

Being truthful does not imply that we should reveal all of our private matters to anybody who is attempting to probe into our affairs. Instead, we should not withhold pertinent information from those who are entitled to an honest response. Being truthful also entails avoiding the many methods that may emerge in order to obtain more than we deserve or to persuade someone to think something about us that is not true. However, there are occasions when some of us may find ourselves in really dangerous circumstances as a result of our candor. When our remarks aren't balanced with kindness, this is frequently the case. The following chapter will look at how that quality may help us avoid many of the issues that might arise from that type of communication.

Kindness is Key

*"Kindness is the language which the deaf can
hear and the blind can see."*

- Mark Twain

Kindness is empathetic, compassionate, thoughtful, polite, and friendly. To make a friend, you must first be one. The phrase "birds of a feather flock together" could not be more accurate. You must be the sort of person that you want to attract; if you want joyful, helpful individuals in your life, you must practice joy and helpfulness. Otherwise, why would anyone want to be around you? Long after the memory of the contact has faded, individuals will remember how the interaction made them feel, as Maya Angelou wisely pointed out.

When we are cruel to others, we make their life far more difficult than they need to be. When we are harsh or disagreeable, we make people feel unwanted, undervalued, and alienated. Would you like to be subjected to such cruelty? Don't you believe treating people badly at work, school, or at home makes your life a lot more difficult than it has to be? Kindness encourages individuals to work together, even if they don't know one other well. It is a lot simpler to surround yourself with individuals who are eager to work with you than it is to try to conquer the world on your own.

Being harsh encompasses a wide range of behaviors. The most prevalent type of unkindness is shown through our words. Unkindness can be viewed as harshness, condescension, or even abruptness. Using your words to degrade others while elevating oneself is not only cruel, but it is also a highly selfish behavior that frequently causes more harm than good. Being courteous is an important component of compassion. Let us spend some time learning more about this lovely characteristic. Being courteous is not as difficult as some people make it out to be. While it is true that being courteous is getting increasingly harder as a result of people's unfavorable views, it is not impossible.

These people's egos may be inflated by being nice, but our politeness is not a reflection of them. Whatever the case may be, being polite reflects well on our character. Polite people are typically perceived as being courteous, ethical, professional, and pleasant. And, in our increasingly linked world, you never know who you could have offended. Consider how humiliated you'll feel if you show up for a job interview only to find out that the man you just cursed in the parking lot because they parked in "your" place is the interviewer. Ask yourself this: would you humiliate others like you have been humiliated? The correct answer is no; you likely understand that people deserve respect. And, for a moment, let's just take that one step further. You also deserve respect. You also deserve kindness.

Everyone has a deep desire for a sense of belonging and being loved. When you help others with this, acknowledging their strengths and weaknesses, they will in turn be kind to you. Likewise, you must learn to love yourself. Begin each day by telling yourself, "I love you." If you accept yourself as you are, eventually you'll become who you want to be. Remember how intrinsically valuable you are! And remember to thank those who compliment you, and compliment yourself when you do good.

Being courteous entails being thoughtful of others' needs, feelings, time, resources, values, and cultural conventions. Being kind and considerate will make you likable, and it will inspire others to do the same. Another advantage of being courteous is that it makes gaining the respect of those around you much easier. They will be obliged to respect you and your values, even if they do not immediately modify their conduct. As a consequence of your efforts, they may change for the better in the future. Isn't it true that life would be so much simpler if we all had jobs where our employees, subordinates, and coworkers treated us with courtesy?

Ignite Forgiveness

*"The weak can never forgive. Forgiveness is the attribute
of the strong."*

- Gandhi

It is difficult to forgive. The fact that we need to use the phrase suggests that we have been harmed in some manner. One of the finest presents you can offer yourself is to forgive a grievance, whether genuine or imagined. This is true whether or not you feel the person merits such compassion. We get bitter when we refuse to forgive. Holding on to hatred is like swallowing poison and expecting the person who harmed us to suffer as a result. It's akin to putting wounds on our bodies and expecting someone else to suffer the consequences. This argument is not just flawed, but also potentially hazardous.

Hatred is suffocating, and resentment may easily turn into hatred. But why is it so difficult for us to forgive? Why does the notion of letting go of the hurt make us feel so uneasy if forgiving someone who has wounded us would be so beneficial? The fundamental issue is that none of us wants to go through the agony of whatever evil has been done to us again. However, when we continue to consider how we were harmed, we unconsciously begin to consider making the individual responsible for their actions. Our faulty sense of justice frequently leads us to assume that if we hang on to all of the sufferings we've caused and refuse to let go, we'll get the justice we deserve. This is especially true if the person does not appear to be remorseful for their actions.

Unfortunately, we can't make someone become a better person by withholding our friendship or kindness. By forcing our thoughts to experience the agony over and over, we are just harming ourselves. Our demeanor, voice, and attitude will be negatively

affected if we are violently storming through life with the burden of anger in our hearts. Regardless of whether or not we have
been harmed by one or a few people, everyone around us will be
affected. We become irritated, sad, and generally nasty as a result
of our resentment. To make matters worse, the people we love, not
the individuals who have mistreated us, are typically the ones who
suffer as a result of what has happened.

Our memory, productivity at work, capacity to execute everyday
activities, ability to focus and even our sex drive have all been
shown to be affected by the weight of resentment. Bitterness and
a refusal to forgive have been related to weaker immune systems,
heart disease, and even high blood pressure. Refusing to forgive,
as you can see, is never a good idea.

But, exactly, what is forgiveness? Is it just a case of forgetting what
happened? Do we just pretend that nothing occurred when we forgive? Nope. That isn't the case. When we forgive, we must do more
than just say sorry. We need to modify the way we think and feel
about others. It's as if we're allowing them to start all over again.
You've decided that you're not going to let the circumstance or the
people involved harm you any longer. It takes a lot of emotional
intelligence, self-control, and love to do this.

Forgiveness entails not just "letting people off the hook" for their
actions, but also allowing individuals involved to move on from
the past and focus on more important matters. It entails filling
oneself with love and radiating that love to others. You must not
cling to the venom or animosity created by the activities that
resulted in the wounds. Being outraged as a result of someone
else's conduct and allowing yourself to be unhappy about it for a
lengthy time is essentially handing over the keys to your happiness to that person. It's as if you're enabling that person to have
complete power over you, and they'll keep doing so until you have
the strength to forgive them.

Forgiveness is also advantageous since it frequently occurs when
we recognize our flaws. When we recall that we, too, have had to

ask for forgiveness many times, it becomes easier for us to for-give. We are not flawless, despite what we may believe. Without recognizing it, we may cause harm to others around us, including those we love. It will be simple for others around us to forgive us when we make mistakes if we refuse to hold grudges and practice forgiveness.

Here are a few reasons why practicing forgiveness is beneficial:

- You will have more peace.
- You will earn the respect of others around you; you will no longer be in agony as a result of the injury, and you will feel less anxious.
- You'll be considerably happy and in a better mood as a result.
- You will have a better night's sleep.
- You'll get more self-control and self-awareness as a result of this program.
- As you become more aware of your unique power, your self-esteem will rise.

Being forgiving does not imply that you must be a pushover who allows oneself to be harmed again. While you will let go of whatever resentment you may have against the person or people who harmed you, you must not put yourself in a position to be wounded in the same manner again. Now that you've seen what these individuals are capable of, it's reasonable to be a bit on edge. However, please exercise extreme caution. When it comes to small transgressions, such as those that were not maliciously commit-ted, don't assume that the act symbolizes who the individual is. Please keep in mind that we all make errors, and we have all caused hurt to others.

Declaring that you've forgiven someone isn't the same as declar-ing that you've gained the "upper hand." The people involved may have done something wrong, but they owe you nothing. Even if they don't apologize, you've gained a lot by making this peace offering and letting go of the animosity that had previously dom-inated you. Remember that you are doing yourself a favor by being forgiving. While they may gain from your choice, forgiving them is a gift to yourself.

The Art of Pardon

We all know how difficult it is to forgive someone who has wronged you, and no one would expect a person to forgive every-one who's wronged you all at once. You may forgive in phases if you want to. Gradually letting go of your animosity toward those who have mistreated you will give you ample time to dig out any traces of hatred you may harbor for them from your mind and heart. If you encounter this individual on a regular basis, you might begin by just saying hello. This may surprise them since they were not anticipating such a kind gesture, and this may open the door for the conversation you both need to resolve. Even though you have been wronged, it is sometimes preferable to take the effort to correct the situation. Always keep in mind how this small action will help you in the long term, regardless of whether they appreciate it or not.

Another easy activity that might help us forgive is putting down the name of the person or people who have harmed us and a list of everything they have ever done to make us unhappy. After you've finished with that list, make a list of all the times you've injured someone and had to ask for forgiveness. This isn't anything that comes to mind when we think about it. Seeing how often our poor behaviors have harmed others around us, especially those we love, may be all the motivation we need to let go of whatever grudges we may hold. Some people are even more alarmed when they find the names of the people they dislike on the list of people they have had to beg forgiveness from.

Making a list of all the positive things this individual has done for you is another beneficial activity. This activity can help you recall that, despite their flaws, this person or these people have a lot of great characteristics. These traits, in the case of people closest to us, are the same reasons why we loved and kept them near in the first place. Consider this: by giving an olive branch of peace, you may be able to assist this individual to recognize the mistake in their thinking and make a positive change. By assisting just one person in becoming a better person, you would have made the world a better place. Such generosity does not go unrecognized or unrewarded.

Consider how much better our lives would be if we didn't have to live each day with the bitterness of anger. One of the most effective methods to recover is to let go of that heavy load. This world is already a disaster, and it doesn't need any more hatred to exacerbate it.

Make Generosity Your Best Friend

"If you can't feed a hundred people, then just feed one."

- Mother Teresa

Charitable people don't need to dole out all of their possessions, although that can be one aspect of generosity. It is also not necessary to be pushed around due to your philanthropy. Being considerate entails, first and foremost, a willingness to offer more than is necessary. Generosity elevates kindness to a new level. You may have a good heart and regularly think about helping others, but you haven't fully perfected the art of generosity until you take the time to start donating your time, energy, or other resources for the benefit of another person.

Generosity motivates us to freely give of ourselves without expecting anything in return. I'm sure you're wondering how donating your possessions may help you live a better life. The reality is that many people consider giving to be one of the keys to happiness in this bleak world. Many medical professionals can attest to the fact that giving is also beneficial to one's health. In reality, these are some of the established advantages of charitable giving:

- Greater happiness as a result of a stronger sense of purpose
- Stronger families and marriages
- Stress relief
- Reduced dementia risk
- You'll be more likely to benefit from the kindness of others if you have a greater appreciation for what you have

A giving individual is always looking for ways to help others. Consider the volunteers that come out every weekend to assist out at soup kitchens. Those of us who are bold enough to join the *Peace Corps* are also thought to be extremely charitable. However, just assisting an old lady with her groceries or pausing to let a youngster cross the street might be deemed charitable. This type of care for others is advantageous because it compels us to concentrate on the needs of others rather than our issues. Anything that reduces the impact of our issues, whether in our personal lives or monetarily, has a direct impact on our health.

Being kind shields us from the cynicism and selfishness that make it so difficult to navigate this world. And it also opens the door for you to get to know people individually! This can lead to some very meaningful friendships, especially if you wait to be generous until after you know what the person would appreciate most. Some individuals enjoy spontaneity, while others want to be asked upfront whether they require assistance. As you learn about the people around you, you will gain insight as to how to bless them most. Hopefully, the kindness and generosity you show will inspire them to be kind and generous to someone else; maybe one day, that kindness will come back to bless you!

Embrace Yourself

"Be yourself; everyone else is already taken." — Oscar Wilde

We all need to rediscover our true identities. This is one of the most important components of effectively navigating through life's disaster. This encouragement does not give you permission to be a jerk. We've previously established that curing ourselves of the suffering produced by this world necessitates a concerted effort to eliminate our bad characteristics. Arrogance, rudeness, dishonesty, and stinginess have no place in your life.

We invite all kinds of negativity into our life when we proudly go about with bad habits. There is only greater anguish and disappointment as a result of this. That's why, in the first chapter, I advised you to get to know yourself. By knowing more about your flaws, you will be more equipped to cure yourself. It necessitates a separation from all of the labels that the world has put on us. These derogatory labels are applied to us because of how we appear, how we dress, or even the place in which we grew up. There's no need for us to let the world force us into a mold that doesn't accurately reflect who we are.

And if you still need some convincing, I've put together five compelling reasons to start being authentic to yourself:

1. It is impossible to please everyone. If you let the people around you define who you are, you'll find yourself continually changing your values in an attempt to please everyone. The only difficulty is that you will wind up failing someone since you will be dealing with so many conflicting expectations. Furthermore, placing oneself under this type of stress will lead to dissatisfaction in the end.

2. You'll find yourself making life-altering decisions depending on the whims of others around you, who will not be affected by your actions. You will be the one to care for that child if you opt to have a child merely because your family feels it's time! If you choose a career because your peers believe you'd be good at it, you'll have to bear the weight of a job you despise for the rest of your

life.

3. The truth is always revealed. If you are lying to yourself, trying to be someone else, people will eventually figure that out. Unfortunately, as we've seen with many superstars, the truth frequently emerges in the form of a major scandal or breakdown.

4. The society in which we live has no idea what it wants. Both the timid housewife and the fiery go-getter are portrayed as ideal women in the media. Men must also be attentive to the requirements of the other sex and the dangerous bad boy, according to society. Which will you be if you let the people around you decide who you are? Whatever you choose to be, keep in mind that putting up a show like this every day is taxing.

5. You will be genuinely happy when you are comfortable with who you are. When you're always pretending to be someone you're not, how can you love yourself? When everything is said and done, if you want to see significant changes, you must take control of your life. If you aren't willing to make dramatic adjustments, you won't get different outcomes. Now is the time to make those adjustments!

People are easier to love, as we can only see their best features or the ones that they choose to show. When you are the only person who sees you for what you appear to the public and understands the inner workings of your brain, which might include some of your most unattractive aspects. It might be difficult to feel motivated to practice self-acceptance.

The act of appreciating your well-being and general happiness is known as loving yourself. It's a willingness to accept unwavering support and self-care. Love of self manifests itself in our desire to satisfy our particular demands. Simple requirements such as cooking when we don't feel like eating, showering when we don't feel like getting out of bed, and so on. Consider the person you care about the most and consider what you would do for them if they were having a poor day. You'd probably do your hardest to assist her to recover her energy and add a good spin on any scenario she's in. Even if you were having a horrible day, you would love her.

So go ahead and do it for yourself. You should love yourself as much as you love others. When you have anxiety, depression, or any other mental health condition or illness, loving yourself might be tough, largely because you don't feel lovable all of the time, but it's still vital. When you're feeling lousy, make yourself a priority.

CONCLUSION: A WATCHED POT NEVER BOILS

Since anxiety and stress are frequently called "a sickness of the twenty-first century," an increasing amount of treatments have been developed. As you've seen in this book, it's possible to live a life free of anxiety and depression. It may take time, but if you are consistent, determined, and patient, you may live a calm and balanced existence. To get to the bottom of your anxiety, you need to figure out what's causing it.

Rather than creating coping techniques, you may strive to lessen, if not eliminate, worry by tackling it at its source, as this book has shown you. It's up to you to seek it out and make an effort to approach situations with an open mind and a good attitude. While this book is jam-packed with tips and tricks, remember to be patient with yourself and focus on one item at a time. You will prevent unneeded tension and strain this way.

Keep your goals in mind and try not to become distracted by all of the "shiny" new techniques you may see. You might be scattered if you try too many approaches at once. It will also prevent you from progressing. Although it's hard, you need to recognize that change does not happen overnight and that you can always seek expert assistance if you believe the work at hand is too large for one person to handle. Asking for help is not a sign of weakness; in fact, admitting that we can't handle everything on our own requires a lot of bravery.

You will gain new abilities and information through being more comfortable with yourself, mind, body, and spirit. This will help you to thrive. The better you understand yourself, the simpler it will be to manage your emotions and embrace them in a way that allows you to heal them. Always remember that emotions are neither good nor evil; they are neutral signals that alert us to something essential that needs to be addressed or repaired.

Emotions may serve as a compass in your life, pointing you in the direction of a harmonious and lovely existence. It may be lengthy and hard, just like any journey, or we may find it a memorable and rewarding experience. Learn to look at each setback as a chance to improve. Remember that everyone learns at their own pace. Comparing yourself to others is a mistake that is made without taking into account all of the important factors. It's easy to forget that everyone begins life differently, and there are those worse off than you. Remember that everyone has different thoughts, goals, and measures of success. Embrace your uniqueness and realize your worth cannot be compared! Don't sell yourself short.

You, despite your challenges with mental health, deserve kindness and an enjoyable life. When you realize this, and strive to achieve peace in your mind and life, you will eventually achieve this goal, and be forever grateful to the past you who believed you were worth it.

I hope you found this book to be useful in helping you gather up the courage to practice some techniques to help yourself. Although progress may be gradual at first, you will never regret your resolve to improve yourself! Every step ahead, no matter how little, is a step forward to positive progress.

REFERENCES

Alves, R. (2021, May 14). *How to Overcome Your Fear of Setting Boundaries.* Essence of Healing Counseling. https://www.essenceofhealingcounseling.com/how-to-overcome-your-fear-of-setting-boundaries/

American Heart Association. (2010). *American Heart Association Recommendations for Physical Activity in Adults and Kids.* Www.heart.org. https://www.heart.org/en/healthy-living/fitness/fitness-basics/aha-recs-for-physical-activity-in-adults

Bhandari, S. (2020, February 18). *Exercise and Depression: Endorphins, Reducing Stress, and More.* WebMD. https://www.webmd.com/depression/guide/exercise-depression#:~:text=When%20you%20exercise%2C%20your%20body

Blinder, D. (2013, June 23). 5 ways pets can ease your stress. TODAY.com; TODAY. https://www.today.com/health/5-ways-pets-can-ease-your-stress-6C10423970

Borst, H. (2021, May 13). *What a change in hormones can do for women's health*. The Checkup. https://www.singlecare.com/blog/female-hormones-and-mental-health/

Bourbeau, L. (2010). *Heal your wounds and find your true self*. Better Yourself Books.

Brewer, J. (2021). *Unwinding anxiety : new science shows how to break the cycles of worry and fear to heal your mind*. Avery, Penguin Random House Llc.

Cherry, K. (2019). *The 6 Types of Basic Emotions and Their Effect on Human Behavior*. Verywell Mind. https://www.verywellmind.com/an-overview-of-the-types-of-emotions-4163976

Chesak, J. (2018, December 10). *The No BS Guide to Setting Healthy Boundaries in Real Life*. Healthline. https://www.healthline.com/health/mental-health/set-boundaries#boundary-basics-and-benefits

Cohen, N. S. (2018). *Advanced methods of music therapy practice : the bonny method of guided imagery and music, Nordoff-Robbins music therapy, analytical music therapy, and vocal psychotherapy*. Jessica Kingsley Publishers.

D'apollonio, D. (2016). *Meditation for beginners : How to relieve stress, anxiety and depression, find inner peace and happiness.* Icg Testing.

DBSA. (n.d.). *8 Tips on Setting Boundaries for Your Mental Health - DBSA.* Depression and Bipolar Support Alliance. Retrieved July 29, 2021, from https://www.dbsalliance.org/support/young-adults/8-tips-on-setting-boundaries-for-your-mental-health/

DJ Mag. (2018, August 17). *Music can reduce anxiety by up to 65%, study shows.* DJMag.com. https://djmag.com/content/music-can-reduce-anxiety-65-study-shows

Fulghum, D. (2008, June 6). *Depression in Women.* WebMD; WebMD. https://www.webmd.com/depression/guide/depression-women

Goleman, D. (2007). *Social intelligence : the new science of human relationships.* Bantam Books.

Gotlin. (2020, November 22). *When the Doctor Becomes the Patient.* Lustgarten Foundation: Pancreatic Cancer Research. https://lustgarten.org/when-the-doctor-becomes-the-patient/

James Whitney Hicks. (2005). *Fifty signs of mental illness : a guide to understanding mental health.* Yale University Press.

Lawler, M. (2020, April 5). What Is Self-Care and Why Is It Critical for Your Health? | Everyday Health. EverydayHealth.com. https://www.everydayhealth.com/self-care/

Matthews, G., Deary, I. J., & Whiteman, M. C. (2009). *Personality traits*. Cambridge University Press.

Miller, K. J., & Rogers, S. A. (2007). *The estrogen-depression connection : the hidden link between hormones & women's depression*. New Harbinger Publications.

Moustakas, C. E. (1974). *Finding yourself, finding others*. Englewood Cliffs, N.J.

National Institute of Mental Health. (2019, February). *NIMH» Major Depression*. Www.nimh.nih.gov. https://www.nimh.nih.gov/health/statistics/major-depression

P Muris. (2007). *Normal and abnormal fear and anxiety in children and adolescents*. Elsevier, Cop.

Podolsky, E. (1954). *Music therapy*. New York, Philosophical Library.

Reader's Digest Association. (2005). *Laughter is the best medicine*. Reader's Digest.

Redding, S. (2020, May 5). *Using Music in Times of Anxiety*. Health-

blog.uofmhealth.org. https://healthblog.uofmhealth.org/
wellness-prevention/using-music-times-of-anxiety

Rosenberg, S. (2017). *Accessing the healing power of the vagus nerve - self-help exercises for an.* North Atlantic Books,U.S.

Sadler, G. (2016, May 14). *Stoicism and Emotions.* Modern Stoicism. https://modernstoicism.com/category/stoicism-and-emotions/

Sommer, C., & Budwine, G. (2014). *Can you help me find my smile?* Advance Publishing, Inc.

Teo, L. (2019, October 17). *The Orange Story.* Medium. https://medium.com/swlh/the-orange-story-8cb9af94e5ad

The World Health Organization. (2021). WHO | What do we mean by self-care? WHO. https://www.who.int/reproductivehealth/self-care-interventions/definitions/en/#:~:text=WHO%20defines%20self%2Dcare%20as

Vanbuskirk, S. (2020, December 10). The Mental Health Benefits of Sunlight. Verywell Mind. https://www.verywellmind.com/the-mental-health-benefits-of-sunlight-5089214

Weir, K. (2011, December). The exercise effect. *Https://Www.apa.org.* https://www.apa.org/monitor/2011/12/

exercise

Wells, D. (2017, March 14). *Anxiety: Breathing Problems and Exercises*. Healthline. https://www.healthline.com/health/anxiety/anxiety-breathing#other-ways-to-manage-anxiety

Wheeler, B. L. (2017). *Music therapy handbook*. The Guilford Press.

Wright, J. H., & Mccray, L. W. (2012). *Breaking free from depression : pathways to wellness*. Guilford Press.

Wurtzel, E. (2017). *Prozac nation : young and depressed in America*. Mariner Books, Houghton Mifflin Harcourt.

Youngs, J. (2002). *Feeling great, looking hot & loving yourself! : health, fitness & beauty for teens*. Scholastic.

Manufactured by Amazon.ca
Bolton, ON

50775478R00046